All About Canada: Table of Contents

Teacher Tips

What I Think I Know / What I Would Like to Know Activity

A great way to engage children in a new theme is to ask them what they think they know about a subject and what they would like to know about a subject. This activity can be completed as a whole group brainstorming session, in cooperative small groups or independently. Once children have had a chance to contemplate the theme, all information is combined to create a class chart that can be displayed in the classroom. Throughout the study, periodically update the children's progress in accomplishing their goal of what they want to know and validate what they think they know.

Morning Messages

Morning Messages are intended to provide students with interesting facts about the theme they are studying while also arranging teachable moments in the use of punctuation. Morning Messages are an excellent way to get the learning going when the students enter in the morning. There are numerous Morning Messages included with this unit. The Morning Messages are written in a letter format. There are several ways to present a Morning Message to your class:

Whole Group: Rewrite the morning message on a large sheet of chart paper and allow students to come look for the "mistakes" in the letter. Then as a whole group read the letter together and use it as a springboard for a class discussion.

Individually: As children enter the classroom, give them a copy of the Morning Message and have them fix the "mistakes". The children practise reading the message with a friend until the class is ready to correct the morning message as a group. Use the Morning Message as a springboard for discussion.

Word List:

Word Lists create a theme related vocabulary. Word Lists should be placed on chart paper for students' reference during writing activities. Encourage students to add theme related words. In addition, classify the word list into the categories of nouns, verbs and adjectives.

Canada Information and Pictures:

Call or email the tourism offices for each of the provinces and territories. They will usually send class packages to support learning. The offices will also send pictures and maps. Travel brochures are also an excellent source of pictures of Canada.

All About Canada: Assessment Strategies

Constructed Response- Learning Logs
Learning logs are an excellent means for children to organize their thoughts and ideas about the science concepts presented. Grammar, spelling or syntax should not be emphasized. The student responses give the teacher opportunities to plan follow up activities that may review and clarify concepts learned.

Learning log entries may be done on a daily basis or intermittently depending on scheduling. Entries should be brief. Time allotted for completion should be less than fifteen minutes. Entries can be done with a whole group, small group or an individual.

Learning logs can include the following kinds of entries:
- Direct instructions by the teacher;
- Key ideas;
- Personal reflections;
- Questions that arise;
- Connections discovered;
- Labeled diagrams and pictures.

Learning logs can take the form of:

- Journals.
- Entries in a classroom portfolio.
- Reflective page.

Student Centered Parent Conferences:
Children have an opportunity to share their portfolio work with their parents.

Self Assessment:
Children are asked to evaluate themselves in different areas such as group skills, oral presentation skills and to reflect on what they learned

Sample Parent Letter

Dear Parents and Guardians,

In our unit of study about Canada, your child will get to know more about the amazing country we live in. By the end of our unit, your child should have an awareness that:

- Canada is made up of provinces, and territories.
- Each province and territory has unique features.
- Canadians come from different places.
- There are famous Canadians.
- There are different kinds of wildlife in Canada.

This unit of study will be used as a springboard for numerous activities including language, arts and crafts.

Families are welcome to contribute to our study by lending any resources, such as CD ROMs, books, travel brochures, collections and tapes.

Your family's enthusiastic participation in our class study is greatly appreciated!

Sincerely,

_____

Research Reporting Opportunities

Research reporting opportunities are an excellent way to ensure children have experience in reading informational text and restating what they have learned in their own words. Set up a theme related centre by preparing a special table with subject related materials including, books, tapes, magazines etc.

When introducing the children to the use of non-fiction books as a source for their research writing, discuss the different parts usually found in a non-fiction book.

The Title Page: Here you will find the book title and the author's name.

The Table of Contents: Here you will find the title of each chapter, what page it starts on and where you can find specific information.

The Glossary: Here you will find the meaning of special words used in the book.

The Index: Here you will find the ABC list of specific topics you can find in the book.

Next, discuss with the children the criteria of a good research project. It should include:

1. Interesting facts
2. The use of proper grammar and punctuation
3. The size of print so that it is easy to read from far away
4. The use of good details in the colouring and the drawing of pictures

Sample Morning Messages

Dear Canadians,

Did you know the early settlers who made Canada their home are known as pioneers? People came to settle in Canada for many different reasons. Some people came to settle here so they could freely practise their religion. Some people settled here because they did not like the way their home countries were run. For the most part, people came to Canada for a better life.

Welcome to Canada!

Dear Canadians,

Did you know that Canada's birthday is on July 1, 1867? When Canada first became a country, there were only four provinces. These provinces were New Brunswick, Nova Scotia, Ontario and Quebec. Now in the year 2003, Canada has ten provinces and three territories.

Happy Birthday Canada!

Sample Morning Messages

Dear Canadians,

Did you know Aboriginal peoples taught pioneers how to take care of sick people? They taught pioneers to make medicine from plants, berries and herbs. They showed pioneers how to use spruce and juniper trees to make a nutritious tea to prevent scurvy.

Thank you!

Dear Canadians,

Did you know Canada's National Anthem was composed for the French-Canadian National Festival? In early 1880, Calixa Lavallée was asked to make a song for the festival that was supposed to be for French-Canadians. Lavallée wrote the music while Adolphe-Basil Routier wrote the French words.

Happy Singing!

All About Canada

Did you know Canada is the second largest country in the world? Canada is found in North America and borders on three oceans. On the west coast is the Pacific Ocean. On the east coast is the Atlantic Ocean. On Canada's northern coast is the Arctic Ocean.

Map of Canada

Colour the province or territory you live in yellow.

Canada and Me

Did you know the only people who are truly from Canada are the Aboriginal peoples?

Other Canadians have ancestors who decided to make Canada their home.

Some Canadians have ancestors from early pioneer times.

Some Canadians are new to Canada.

Think about it!

I was born in _____

I live in _____

I live in the province or territory of

_____

I like living here because ....

_____

_____

Create A Family Tree

Trace how far back your family tree can go!

Where were you born? _____

From what parts of the world is your family from?

_____

_____

_____

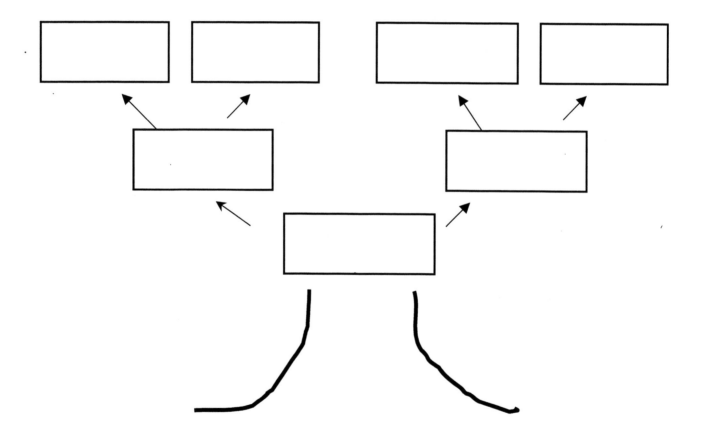

Share your finding with your classmates.

Aboriginal Peoples and Pioneers
Farming

- Aboriginal peoples showed pioneers how to farm.

- Aboriginal peoples taught pioneers how to plant crops like corn, pumpkins, beans and squash.

- Aboriginal peoples taught pioneers how to make the soil rich with fish fertilizer.

- Aboriginal peoples showed pioneers how to make flour for cornmeal.

Aboriginal Peoples and Pioneers
Surviving Cold Winters

- Aboriginal peoples taught pioneers how to survive cold winters.

- Aboriginal peoples traded goods for warm outer clothing.

- Aboriginal peoples made warm clothes and special shoes called moccasins using deerskin or other animal hides.

- Aboriginal peoples showed pioneers how to make snowshoes to help walk in snow.

- Aboriginal peoples showed pioneers how to make toboggans.

Thinking about:
Aboriginal Peoples and Pioneers

Complete the chart using information from the reading cards.

Ways Aboriginal Peoples Helped Pioneers	Example
Farming	
Living in the winter	

Name _____

History of Canada

Did you know Canada's birthday is on **July 1, 1867**? When Canada first became a country, there were only four provinces. These provinces were **New Brunswick**, **Nova Scotia**, **Ontario** and **Quebec**. When these provinces joined, it was called **confederation**. Now Canada has **ten** provinces and **three** territories.

Canada has a **prime minister**. The prime minister's job is to run the country. Canada's first prime minister was **Sir John A. Macdonald**. Canada also recognizes the British Queen as Canada's Queen.

Answer the following questions from the reading:

1. When is Canada's birthday?

_____

2. What were the first four provinces in Canada?

_____   _____

_____   _____

3. Whose job is it to run the country?

_____

Name _____

Write a letter to the Prime Minister

Did you know you can a write a letter to the prime minister and not use a stamp? Write a letter to the prime minister of Canada. Make sure you thank the prime minister in advance for a reply.

Address: Right Honourable _____
           Prime Minister
           House of Commons
           Ottawa, Ontario
           Canada

Here are some ideas to write about in your letter:

- Tell about where you live.
- Tell about where you go to school.
- Tell about why you are proud to be Canadian.
- Ask questions about Canada or the government.
- Draw a picture to add to your letter.

    ✓ Remember to check for capitals and periods.
    ✓ Remember to print neatly.
    ✓ Remember to check for spelling.

Province and Territory Information Cards

British Columbia

- British Columbia is a western province.

- British Columbia's capital city is Victoria.

- British Columbia's flower is the pacific dogwood.

- British Columbia is known for the Rocky and Coastal Mountains, and Whistler Mountain.

- A famous person from British Columbia is Rick Hansen. He is an athlete who raised lots of money for charity.

Northwest Territories

- The Northwest Territories is one of three territories.

- The Northwest Territories' capital city is Yellowknife.

- The Northwest Territories' flower is the mountain avens.

- The Northwest Territories is known for its lakes, and Caribou festival.

- A famous person from the Northwest Territories is Nellie Cournoyea. She is a politician.

Province and Territory Information Cards

Yukon

- The Yukon is the smallest territory in Canada.

- The Yukon's capital city is Whitehorse.

- The Yukon's flower is the fireweed.

- The Yukon is known for the Klondike Gold Rush in 1896.

- A famous person from the Yukon is Pierre Berton. He is a writer.

Nunavut

- Nunavut is Canada's newest and biggest territory.

- Nunavut's capital city is the Iqaluit.

- Nunavut's flower is the arctic poppy.

- Nunavut is known for its Toonik Tyme spring carnival, Baffin Island, and Ellesmere Island.

- A famous person from the Nunavut is Pitseolak Ashoona. She was an Inuit artist who created sculptures and prints.

Province and Territory Information Cards

Nova Scotia

- Nova Scotia is an Atlantic province.

- Nova Scotia's capital city is Halifax.

- Nova Scotia's flower is the mayflower.

- Nova Scotia is known for its rocky coastline, and lobsters.

- The ship shown on the Canadian dime was made in Nova Scotia.
- A famous person from Nova Scotia is Alexander Graham Bell. He invented the telephone.

New Brunswick

- New Brunswick is an Atlantic province.

- New Brunswick's capital city is Fredericton.

- New Brunswick's flower is the purple violet.

- New Brunswick is known for a rocky coastline, Rocks Provincial Park, Grand Manan Island and potatoes.

- A famous person from New Brunswick is Gilbert Ganong. He was a candy maker.

Province and Territory Information Cards

Newfoundland and Labrador

- Newfoundland and Labrador is an Atlantic province.

- The capital city is St. John's.

- The flower is the pitcher plant.

- Newfoundland and Labrador is known for its icebergs, the Grand Banks, and a long coastline.

- A famous person from Newfoundland and Labrador is Christopher Pratt. He is an artist.

Prince Edward Island

- Prince Edward Island is an Atlantic province.

- Prince Edward Island's capital city is Charlottetown.

- Prince Edward Island's flower is the lady's slipper.

- Prince Edward Island is known for Cavendish Beach, Green Gables House, potatoes and Confederation Bridge.

- A famous person from Prince Edward Island is Lucy Maud Montgomery. She was a writer.

Province and Territory Information Cards

Ontario

- Ontario is a province.

- Ottawa, Ontario is the capital of Canada.

- Ontario's capital city is Toronto.

- Ontario's flower is the trillium.

- Ontario is known for the CN Tower, Niagara Falls, and the Niagara fruit belt.

- A famous person from Ontario is Wayne Gretsky. He is a hockey player.

Quebec

- Quebec is Canada's largest province.

- Quebec's capital city is Quebec City.

- Quebec's flower is the white lily.

- Quebec is known for the winter carnival, its maple syrup, and for making electricity.

- A famous person from Quebec is Pierre Elliot Trudeau. He was a prime minister of Canada.

Province and Territory Information Cards

Manitoba

- Manitoba is a Prairie province.

- Manitoba's capital city is Winnipeg.

- Manitoba's flower is the prairie crocus.

- Manitoba is known for wheat, the Royal Canadian Mint and polar bears.

- A famous person from Manitoba is Louis Riel. He was often called the "Father of Manitoba".

Saskatchewan

- Saskatchewan is a Prairie province.

- Saskatchewan's capital city is Regina.

- Saskatchewan's flower is the prairie lily.

- Saskatchewan is known for the "Snowbirds", uranium, potash, wheat and farming.

- A famous person from Saskatchewan is Jeanne Sauve. She was the first woman to become Governor General of Canada.

Province and Territory Information Cards

Alberta

- Alberta is a Prairie province.

- Alberta's capital city is Edmonton.

- Alberta's flower is the wild rose.

- Alberta is known for the Columbia Icefield, Banff National Park, Calgary Stampede, ranches, Dinosaur Provincial Park and the West Edmonton Mall.

- A famous person from Alberta is Douglas Cardinal. He was one of the first architects to use computers.

Create a Travel Poster

Travel posters help convince people to go places. Create a poster to convince someone to visit a province, territory or Canada.

Make sure you include:
- the destination.
- interesting facts and things to do.
- a picture and neat printing.

Alberta

Did you know Alberta is the fourth largest province in Canada? Alberta is a Prairie province. Alberta's capital city is Edmonton.

Alberta is known for its large mountain range called the Rocky Mountains. In Alberta, there is the Columbia Icefield in Banff and Jasper National Parks. An ice field is made of large pieces of ice left over from the ice age millions of years ago.

In Alberta, there are lots of farms and cattle ranches. Some farm crops are wheat, oats and barley. Alberta is also the main producer of oil, natural gas, and coal in Canada.

A good time to visit Alberta is during the Calgary Stampede in July. The Calgary Stampede is a rodeo festival that has bull riding, calf roping and wagon racing. The West Edmonton Mall in Edmonton is the biggest mall in the world. It has over 800 stores!

Dinosaur Provincial Park is in Alberta. This is a great place to see dinosaur bones. The Royal Tyrell Museum near Drumheller has the biggest display of dinosaur bones in the world.

A famous person from Alberta is Douglas Cardinal. He was one of the first architects to use computers to design buildings. He has won many awards.

Thinking about: Alberta

Match the phrases to make true sentences.

1. Alberta is known for its large mountain range

2. In Alberta, there are lots

3. The Calgary Stampede

4. The Royal Tyrell Museum near Drumheller has

5. In Alberta, there is the Columbia Icefield

6. Alberta's capital city

is a rodeo festival.

the biggest display of dinosaur bones.

called the Rocky Mountains.

is Edmonton.

of farms and cattle ranches.

in Banff and Jasper National Parks.

What are three interesting facts about Alberta?

1. _____

_____

2. _____

_____

3. _____

_____

British Columbia

Did you know British Columbia is the third largest province in Canada? British Columbia is a western province. British Columbia has a mainland and many small islands. These islands include Vancouver Island and the Queen Charlotte Islands. British Columbia's capital city is Victoria.

British Columbia is known for its mountain ranges. They are the Rocky Mountains and the Coast Mountains. British Columbia has one of the largest rivers in Canada called the Fraser River. British Columbia also has some of the largest and oldest trees in Canada.

British Columbia has good land for farming. The Okanagan Valley is known for growing fruit like apples, plums and cherries.

There is lots of wildlife in British Columbia. At the Gwaii Haana National Park Reserve, there are whales and seabirds. At Yoho National Park, there are grizzly bears and cougars. British Columbia is also famous for fishing. There are lots of fish like salmon, halibut, clam, cod, oysters, shrimp, crab, and herring.

A good place to visit in British Columbia is Stanley Park in Vancouver. At Stanley Park, there is an aquarium, beaches, hiking trails and totem poles. People also like to visit Whistler Mountain to ski.

Thinking about: British Columbia

Match the phrases to make true sentences.

1. British Columbia has a	for fishing.
2. The Okanagan Valley is	are mountain ranges.
3. British Columbia has some of	mainland and many small islands.
4. British Columbia is famous	known for growing fruit.
5. The Rocky Mountains and the Coast Mountains	a western province.
6. British Columbia is a province	the largest and oldest trees in Canada.

What are three interesting facts about British Columbia?

1. _____

_____

2. _____

_____

3. _____

_____

Totem Poles

The First Nations people carved figures into poles a sign of their history. These special poles made from cedar trunks are called totem poles. Carvings of animal spirits on the poles helped to tell the history of a village or family. Some examples of spirits are a beaver, bear, wolf, whale, raven, eagle or frog. Totem Poles were also used as welcoming posts or as memorials for the dead.

Create a totem pole in the following activity.

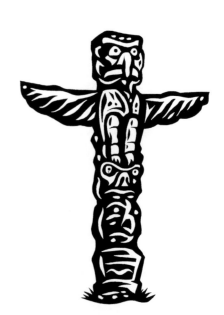

What you need:
Paper tubes
Construction paper
Glue
Colouring materials
Scissors

What to do:
1. Introduce to students how animal spirit figures were carved in totem poles.
2. Demonstrate how to draw wings on a piece of paper.
3. Show how to add details on the shape of the wing to represent geometric designs, using colouring materials.
4. Demonstrate for students how to design totem faces or spirits, colouring details.
5. Next, cover the paper tube with brown construction paper, gluing it in place.
6. Then have students cut out their wings and faces and glue them to the front of the paper tube.

Ontario

Did you know the name Ontario comes from an Iroquoian word, meaning "beautiful lake"? Ontario became a province on July 1, 1867.

More than one third of Canada's population lives in the province of Ontario. The capital city of Ontario is Toronto. Toronto is the largest city in Canada. Many people choose to live in southern and western Ontario.

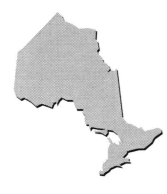

Ontario's nickname is "the Heartland of Canada". Rocks, forests, rivers and lakes cover half of Ontario. The Niagara fruitbelt is known for growing fruit like grapes, peaches, and apples.

Many people also enjoy hiking, rafting and camping at Ontario provincial parks. People also go visit Canada's capital city Ottawa, Toronto's CN Tower, and Niagara Falls.

A famous person from Ontario is Wayne Gretsky. He is a hockey player. Wayne Gretsky scored more than 1000 goals during his hockey career. He has won the Order of Canada award.

Thinking about: Ontario

Match the phrases to make true sentences.

1. The name Ontario comes from an Iroquoian word,

2. The capital city of Ontario

3. Toronto is the largest

4. Rocks, forests, rivers and lakes

5. A famous person from Ontario

6. The Niagara fruitbelt is known

for growing fruit like grapes, peaches and apples.

cover half of Ontario.

is Toronto.

is Wayne Gretsky.

city in Canada.

meaning "beautiful lake".

What are three interesting facts about Ontario?

1. _____

_____

2. _____

_____

3. _____

_____

Nunavut

Did you know Nunavut means "our land" in the Inuit language, Inuktitut? Nunavut became Canada's newest territory on April 1, 1999. Nunavut used to be a part of the Northwest Territories. Iqaluit is the capital city of Nunavut. Most people who live in Nunavut are Inuit.

Nunavut is the biggest territory in Canada. Seven of Canada's biggest islands such as Baffin Island are found there. Even though Nunavut is a big place, the population is very small. Some wildlife found in Nunavut include: caribou, polar bears, muskox, Atlantic walrus, reindeer, and fish like lake trout or arctic char.

Most of the land in Nunavut is frozen much of the year. This is why Nunavut's growing season is very short and the plants are small. Nunavut has less precipitation than areas of the Sahara Desert. Hunting and fishing are an important part of life in Nunavut.

Snowmobiles are one of the main ways to travel in Nunavut. Airplanes bring food, dairy products, machinery and people to areas where it is difficult to travel. In Nunavut, almost every community has its own airport!

A famous person from Nunavut is Pitseolak Ashoona. She was an Inuit artist who made drawings, prints and sculptures. She received the Order of Canada in 1977.

Thinking about: Nunavut

Name _____

Match the phrases to make true sentences.

1. Nunavut means "our land"   is frozen much of the year.

2. Nunavut became Canada's newest   populated places on Earth.

3. Most of the land in Nunuvut   in the Inuit language, Inuktitut.

4. Nunavut is one the least   a part of the Northwest Territories.

5. Iqaluit is the capital   territory on April 1, 1999.

6. Nunavut used to be   city of Nunavut.

What are three interesting facts about Nunavut?

1. _____

_____

2. _____

_____

3. _____

_____

Quebec

Did you know Quebec is the largest province in Canada? Quebec's capital city is Quebec City. Many people in Quebec speak French.

Quebec has lots of water. Quebec makes most of Canada's electricity at large hydroelectric power plants like the one in James Bay.

Did you know Quebec has the largest forest in Canada? Quebec is known for making paper, boxes, tissue and newsprint. People across Canada use Quebec's lumber to build things like homes.

Quebec is famous for its maple syrup. Quebec has many maple tree farms. Quebec also grows apples, vegetables, strawberries, raspberries and blueberries. Quebec has many dairy farms too.

A good time to visit Quebec is February. Every year Quebec City has a famous winter carnival that lasts ten days. People can play winter sports, go to dances and see ice sculptures and parades. At the winter carnival there is a mascot named "Bonhomme Carnaval."

A famous person from Quebec is Pierre Elliot Trudeau. He was a Prime Minister of Canada of Canada for more than fifteen years. He was known for making Canada's official languages both English and French. He also helped Canada gain control over its constitution.

Thinking about Quebec:

Match the phrases to make true sentences.

1. Quebec is the largest   speak French.

2. Quebec has the   its maple syrup.

3. Quebec is famous for   winter carnival every year.

4. Quebec makes most of   province in Canada.

5. Most people in Quebec   largest forest in Canada.

6. Quebec City has a famous   Canada's electricity at large hydroelectric power plants.

What are three interesting facts about Quebec?

1. _____

_____

2. _____

_____

3. _____

_____

Whole Group Activity:
Bonhomme Carnaval Ice Sculptures

What you need:
- water
- food colouring in a variety of colours
- different moulds such as small cube trays, shapes etc.
- snow
- pitchers for each of the food colouring

What to do:
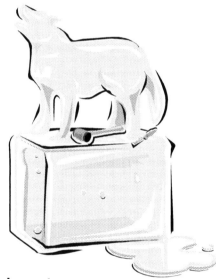

1. Demonstrate for the children how to mix water and food colouring in a pitcher.
2. Model for the children how to carefully fill the various moulds.
3. Place the moulds in the freezer. Encourage the children to predict what they think will happen to the coloured water.
4. After the coloured water has frozen, let the frozen mould slightly thaw in order to remove easily
5. Outside in the designated area, have children create an icy structure using the moulded coloured ice and snow for mortar.
6. Encourage children to be creative and talk about their sculpture.

Saskatchewan

Did you know Saskatchewan is the fifth largest province in Canada? Saskatchewan is a Prairie province. Saskatchewan's capital city is Regina. Saskatchewan is home to many Metis, Aboriginal peoples and other people from around the world. Most people in Saskatchewan speak English.

Did you know Saskatchewan has the most farmland in Canada? Saskatchewan is known for growing wheat. People across Canada and the world buy wheat from Saskatchewan. Saskatchewan's nickname is Canada's "breadbasket".

Did you know Saskatchewan's city of Moose Jaw has the largest jet pilot training base in Canada? The Canadian Forces jet flying team called the "Snowbirds" is famous all over the world. The "Snowbirds" are military pilots who can make their jets do tricks in the air.

A famous person from Saskatchewan is Jeanne Sauve (1922-1993). She was a politician and writer. In 1984, Jeanne Sauve was the first woman to become the governor general of Canada. The job of governor general is to be the representative of the Queen to the Canadian Government.

Thinking about: Saskatchewan

Match the phrases to make true sentences.

1. Saskatchewan is   buy wheat from Saskatchewan.

2. Saskatchewan has the   make their jets do tricks in the air.

3. People across Canada and the world   a prairie province.

4. Moose Jaw has the largest   Canada's "breadbasket".

5. The "Snowbirds" are pilots who can   most farmland in Canada.

6. Saskatchewan's nickname is   jet pilot training base in Canada.

What are three interesting facts about Saskatchewan?

1. _____

   _____

2. _____

   _____

3. _____

   _____

Manitoba

Did you know Manitoba is the fifth smallest province in Canada? Manitoba is a Prairie province. Manitoba's capital city is Winnipeg. Manitoba is home to many Metis, Aboriginal peoples and other people from around the world. Many people in Manitoba speak English and French.

Manitoba is the geographic centre of Canada. Manitoba's nickname is the "keystone" province. Lakes and large rivers cover a lot of Manitoba's land.

A place to visit in Manitoba is the Royal Canadian Mint in Winnipeg. This is where coins are made for Canada and other countries around the world. Churchill Manitoba, a deep-sea port in Hudson Bay is the  world's largest place to see polar bears. The Royal Winnipeg Ballet is a famous dance company that tours across Canada.

A famous person from Manitoba is Louis Riel. He was often called the "Father of Manitoba".

Thinking about Manitoba

Match the phrases to make true sentences.

1. Many people in Manitoba   the "keystone" province.

2. A place to visit in Manitoba is   the world's largest place to see
                                     polar bears.

3. Manitoba's capital city   speak English and French.

4. Manitoba's nickname is   prairie province.

5. Churchill Manitoba, a deep-sea   is Winnipeg.
   port in Hudson Bay is

6. Manitoba is a   the Royal Canadian Mint in
                                     Winnipeg.

What are three interesting facts about Manitoba?

1. _____

_____

2. _____

_____

3. _____

_____

Yukon

Did you know the Yukon is the smallest territory in Canada? The Yukon's capital city is Whitehorse. Old Crow is the only settlement in the Yukon, north of the Arctic Circle.

The Yukon has the highest mountain in Canada. It is called Mount Logan. The Yukon has many lakes and streams. They are filled with fish including, salmon, whitefish, lake trout, rainbow trout, arctic char, and northern pike.

The Yukon has lots of natural resources like gold, silver, lead, zinc and oil. The Yukon also has a large fur trapping industry. Beaver, lynx, muskrat, fox and wolverine are some of the animals trapped for their furs.

Many people like to visit the Yukon. In the Yukon you can hike, raft, rock climb, fish and enjoy other outdoor things. People also like to visit, "the Signpost Forest" at Watson Lake. There are over 30 000 signs from around the world that make up "the Signpost Forest"

A famous person from the Yukon is Pierre Berton. He is a famous writer. Pierre Berton has written many books like The Secret World of Og.

Thinking about: The Yukon

Match the phrases to make true sentences.

1. The Yukon is the   highest mountain in Canada.

2. Yukon's capital city   many lakes and streams.

3. The Yukon has the   "the Signpost Forest" at
                                       Watson Lake.

4. The Yukon has   north of the Arctic Circle.

5. Old Crow is a settlement   smallest territory in Canada.

6. People like to visit,   is Whitehorse.

What are three interesting facts about Yukon?

1. _____

   _____

2. _____

   _____

3. _____

   _____

Thinking about: The Yukon

Visitors love to go see, "The Signpost Forest" in the Yukon. In the space below, make a your own forest of signs.

There are all kinds of signs. See how many different kinds you can make for your sign forest.

Northwest Territories

Did you know the Northwest Territories is the second largest territory in Canada? Yellowknife is the capital city of the Northwest Territories.

The Dene and Inuit were the first people to live in the Northwest Territories. Most people now live in the Mackenzie River Valley.

The Northwest Territories is known for its water. It has the longest river in Canada, the Mackenzie River. It has the deepest lake in Canada, Great Slave Lake. It has one the largest lakes in Canada, Great Bear Lake.

Some animals found in the Northwest Territories include bison, caribou, musk oxen, peregrine falcons and many more!

The nickname for the Northwest Territories is "the Land of the Midnight sun." If you visit the Northwest Territories, you may be able to see the Northern lights or the Aurora Borealis.

A famous person from the North West Territories is Nellie Cournoyea. She is a politician. Nellie Cournoyea was the first Aboriginal woman to be elected government leader for the North West Territories. She has also won the National Aboriginal Achievement Award.

Thinking about:
Northwest Territories

Name _____

Match the phrases to make true sentences.

1. The Dene and Inuit were	of the Northwest Territories.
2. Yellowknife is the capital city	is the longest river in Canada.
3. The nickname for the Northwest Territories is	to be elected government leader.
4. The Mackenzie river	the first people to live in the Northwest Territories.
5. Great Slave Lake.	"the Land of the Midnight sun."
6. Nellie Cournoyea was the first Aboriginal woman	is the deepest lake in Canada.

What are three interesting facts about The Northwest Territories?

1. _____

_____

2. _____

_____

3. _____

_____

Aurora Borealis

Did you know Canada's Northern lights are famous? The Aurora Borealis or Northern Lights is something that glows and flickers in the night sky around the Arctic North Pole at a certain time of year. It looks like a curtain of pale red light that slowly comes over the horizon and turns into a lovely green colour. Eventually you can see spots of both red and green.

The Aurora Borealis is created because of the interaction between the earth's magnetic field and the earth's atmosphere. In the following activity, create your own Aurora Borealis.

What you need:

- black construction paper
- red, green, tempera paint
- sparkles
- newspaper

What to do:

1. Lay black construction paper on the newspaper;
2. Using a spoon carefully drip red and green paint onto construction paper, until most of paper is covered;
3. Next place a second piece of black construction paper on top;
4. Twist the second piece of black construction paper by laying your hand over the paper and rotating;
5. Pull the papers apart and sprinkle with sparkles for an "Aurora Borealis" effect.

Think about it!

Learn more about the Aurora Borealis and see real pictures on the following web sites:
http://www2.polarnet.com/~hutch/aurora.html
http://climate.gi.alaska.edu/Curtis/aurora/aurora.html

Nova Scotia

Did you know Nova Scotia is the second smallest province? Nova Scotia is an Atlantic Province. It has two parts: the mainland and Cape Breton Island. Halifax is the capital city of Nova Scotia.

Nova Scotia is surrounded by the Atlantic Ocean, the Bay of Fundy and the Northumberland Strait. Nova Scotia has many little islands and a rocky coastline.

Did you know Nova Scotia is known as Canada's ocean playground? A place to visit in Nova Scotia is Peggy's Cove. Peggy's Cove is a small fishing village. Peggy's Cove has a lighthouse, which is now a post office.

Another place to visit is Lunenburg, a world heritage site. It has three hundred year old buildings. Lunenburg is where the Bluenose II ship was built. See a picture of the Bluenose II on the back of the Canadian dime.

Did you know people across Canada like to eat Nova Scotia's lobsters? Other fish in Nova Scotia are scallops, crabs, clams, salmon, pollock, herring and haddock. Some animals in Nova Scotia are whales, bald eagles, moose and turtles.

A famous person from Nova Scotia is Alexander Graham Bell. He invented the telephone.

Thinking about: Nova Scotia

Match the phrases to make true sentences.

1. Nova Scotia has two parts:　　a small fishing village.

2. Nova Scotia is　　to eat Nova Scotia's lobsters.

3. Nova Scotia has many little islands　　the mainland and Cape Breton Island.

4. Peggy's Cove is　　invented the telephone.

5. People across Canada like　　an Atlantic province.

6. Alexander Graham Bell　　and a rocky coastline.

What are three interesting facts about Nova Scotia?

1. _____

_____

2. _____

_____

3. _____

_____

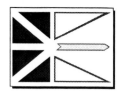

Newfoundland and Labrador

Did you know Newfoundland and Labrador is the most eastern province in Canada? It is an Atlantic Province whose nickname is "the rock". It has two parts: the island of Newfoundland and the mainland of Labrador. The capital city is St. John's. Newfoundland and Labrador was the last province to join Canada.

Newfoundland can be reached by airplane or ferryboat. Newfoundland is surrounded by the Gulf of St. Lawrence, the Atlantic Ocean, and the Arctic Ocean. Newfoundland has a long coastline and many little islands.

Did you know Newfoundland is famous for its cod? The Grand Banks of Newfoundland is one of the most famous fishing areas in the world. Fish in Newfoundland include Atlantic salmon, flounder, turbot, halibut, bluefin tuna, haddock, herring and redfish. Lobster, scallops, shrimps and crab are also found there.

Most people in Newfoundland live in small fishing villages. There are icebergs in the ocean near Newfoundland most of the year.

A famous person from Newfoundland is Christopher Pratt. He is an artist known around the world. Many of his paintings are of rooms or buildings.

Thinking about: Newfoundland

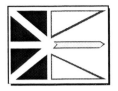

Match the phrases to make true sentences.

1. The capital city   live in small fishing villages.

2. Newfound has a long coastline   the ocean near Newfoundland.

3. Most people in Newfoundland   is St. John's.

4. Newfoundland is famous   by airplane or ferryboat.

5. There are ice burgs in   and many little islands.

6. Newfoundland can be reached   for its cod.

What are three interesting facts about Newfoundland?

1. _____

_____

2. _____

_____

3. _____

_____

Name _____

Thinking about: Newfoundland

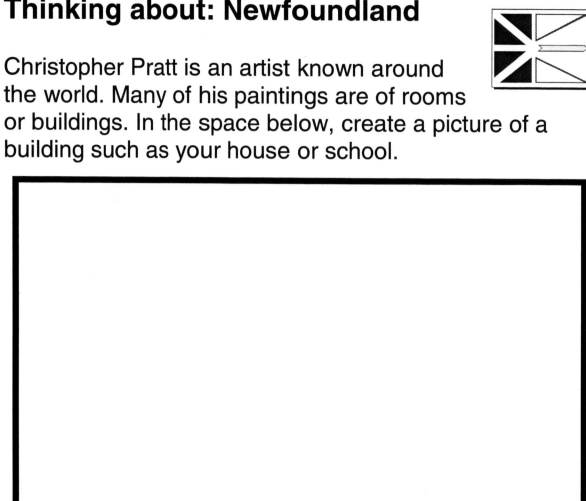

Christopher Pratt is an artist known around the world. Many of his paintings are of rooms or buildings. In the space below, create a picture of a building such as your house or school.

Write a sentence about your picture.

_____

New Brunswick

Did you know New Brunswick is the third smallest province? New Brunswick is an Atlantic province. New Brunswick has a mainland and many islands. It is surrounded by water on two sides. The capital city of New Brunswick is Fredericton. Many people in New Brunswick speak English and French. New Brunswick is the only province in Canada that is bilingual!

Did you know New Brunswick has the longest covered bridge in the world? The Hartland Bridge was built in 1921 and is 390 metres long.

A place to visit in New Brunswick is the Rocks Provincial Park on the Bay of Fundy. People come to see the tall rocks that have trees growing on top. People also go there to hike, kayak and see the highest tides in the world.

Did you know New Brunswick's Saint John River Valley is called the "potato belt"? This is because people across Canada eat potatoes from New Brunswick. New Brunswick also grows apples, strawberries, blueberries and cranberries.

A famous person from New Brunswick is Gilbert Ganong (1851-1917). He is a famous Canadian candy maker. In 1885, he created a candy called the chicken bone. The chicken bone is a cinnamon-flavoured hard candy filled with chocolate inside.

Thinking about: New Brunswick

Match the phrases to make true sentences.

1. New Brunswick has   called the "Potato Belt".

2. The capital city of New Brunswick   a mainland and many islands.

3. New Brunswick has the longest   by water by two sides.

4. New Brunswick's Saint John River Valley is   on the Bay of Fundy.

5. New Brunswick is surrounded   covered bridge in the world.

6. The Rocks Provincial Park is   is Fredericton.

What are three interesting facts about New Brunswick.

1. _____

_____

2. _____

_____

3. _____

_____

Prince Edward Island

Did you know Prince Edward Island is the smallest province in Canada? Prince Edward Island is an Atlantic Province. The capital city of Prince Edward Island is Charlottetown.

Prince Edward Island is 224 kilometres long and surrounded on three sides by the Gulf of St. Lawrence. Prince Edward Island has many sandy beaches and sand dunes.

Did you know Confederation Bridge joins Prince Edward Island and New Brunswick? Confederation Bridge opened in 1997 and is almost 13kilometres long. People travel by ferryboat from Nova Scotia to Prince Edward Island.

Did you know Prince Edward Island is famous for its oysters? Prince Edward Island has many oyster farms in Malpeque Bay. Prince Edward Island also has lobsters, clams, scallops, and mussels. Fish like herring, tuna and mackerel are found there too.

A famous person from Prince Edward Island is Lucy Maud Montgomery. She is famous for writing the book called Anne of Green Gables. This book is about a girl growing up in Prince Edward Island. People from around the world come to visit Green Gables house in Prince Edward Island.

Name _____

Thinking about:
Prince Edward Island

Match the phrases to make true sentences.

1. Prince Edward Island is

2. The capital city of Prince Edward Island

3. Confederation Bridge joins

4. Prince Edward Island is famous

5. People from around the world

6. Prince Edward Island is

Prince Edward Island and New Brunswick.

come to visit Green Gables house.

for its oysters.

the smallest province in Canada.

an Atlantic Province.

is Charlottetown.

What are three interesting facts about Prince Edward Island?

1. _____

_____

2. _____

_____

3. _____

_____

Capital City Match Up

Match the Provinces to the names of their capital cities.

Alberta	Toronto
British Columbia	Halifax
Quebec	Fredericton
Ontario	Edmonton
Saskatchewan	Winnipeg
Manitoba	Quebec City
Nova Scotia	Whitehorse
New Brunswick	Victoria
New Foundland and Labrador	Regina
North West Territories	St. John
Prince Edward Island	Iqaluit
Nunavut	Yellowknife
Yukon	Charlottetown

Canada's Official Languages

Did you know Canada has two official languages? These two languages are English and French.

Canada's National Anthem   (English Version)

O Canada! Our home and native land.
True Patriot love in all thy sons command.
With glowing hearts we thee rise.
The true North strong and free!
From far and wide, O Canada,
We stand on guard for thee.

God keep our land glorious and free!
O Canada, we stand on guard for
thee.
O Canada we stand guard for thee.

Canada's National Anthem (French Version)

O Canada, terre de nos aieux
Ton fron est ceint de fleurons glorieux
Car ton bras sait porter l'epee
Il sait porter la croix;
Ton histoirie est une epopee

Des plus brilliants exploits
Et ta valeur, de foi trempee
Protegera nos foyers et nos droits
Protegera nos foyers et nos droits

Learn the French words for colours!

* green- vert   *blue -bleu   * purple-violet   * brown-brun

* red- rouge   * orange- orange   * black-noir   * yellow- jaune

vert	brun	jaune	orange	brun
rouge	violet	bleu	vert	violet
orange	jaune	rouge	noir	bleu
bleu	vert	orange	violet	noir
noir	brun	vert	rouge	jaune

Canadian Post Card

Pretend you have visited a province, territory or special place in Canada. Write a post card to tell about your visit. Cut out the two parts of your post card and paste together. "Mail" the postcard to a friend in the class!

To:

_____

_____

_____

Design A Canadian Stamp

Design a stamp that symbolizes Canada in the space below.

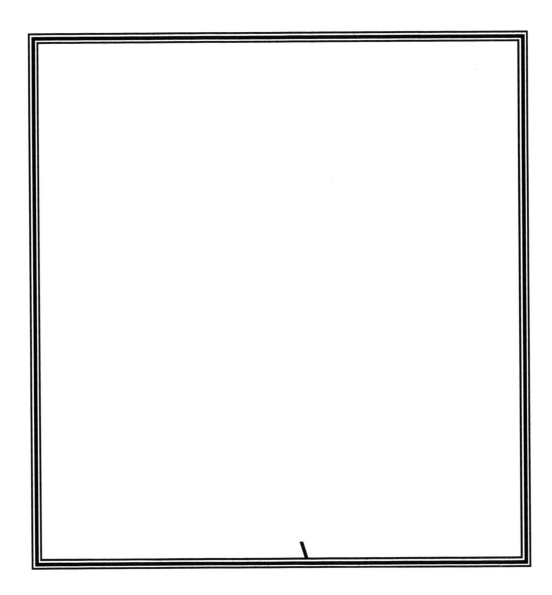

Tell about your stamp:

_____

_____

Canada's Flag

Maple Leaf Tracers

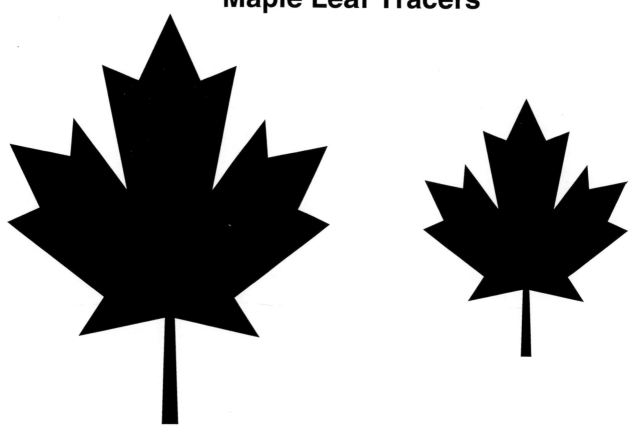

The Canada Goose

Did you know the Canada goose is a symbol of Canada? The Canada goose is a special bird. These birds like to fly in the shape of a "V". This helps them from getting too tired on long journeys.

Colour and cut the Canada geese below and paste them into the shape of a "V" on a separate piece of paper.

The Royal Canadian Mounted Police

Did you know the Royal Canadian Mounted Police are known as Mounties?

- The Royal Canadian Mounted Police is Canada's national police service.

- The Mounties have been around since 1873.

- The Mounties are known for 'always getting their man' and are a symbol of Canada.

- The men and women who are our Mounties are famous around the world.

The Royal Canadian Mounted Police still wear their uniforms on special occasions and parades.

Colour the following;

Coat: bright red
Hat: tan with a black band
Boots: brown
Belt: black
Buttons: yellow
Pants: black with yellow stripes on the sides

Canada's Beaver

Did you know the beaver is one of Canada's national symbols? Early explorers from Europe admired the beautiful fur of the beaver. They brought beaver pelts back to Europe. The people in Europe loved the beaver fur and this was the beginning of the fur trade in Canada. Draw your own Canadian beaver!

Some of Canada's Symbols

The Maple Leaf

- The maple leaf is on Canadian money that was made between the years 1876 and 1901.

- Some regiments of Canada's army, use the maple leaf on their badges.

- The Royal Arms of Canada, the crest Canada uses around the world, has three maple leaves on it.

- The Canadian flag has a big red maple leaf in the centre of a white square and red sides.

The Moose

- Moose are found everywhere in Canadian forests, and their picture can be found on the back of a quarter.

- The moose is an herbivore and it loves to nibble juicy leaves, twigs and plants. The moose loves to swim. Its favourite treat is water lilies.

- A bull or male moose can weigh as much as six wrestlers, and stand taller that most men!

- Only bull moose have antlers. Females, or cows are smaller than bulls, but they still can be as big as a large horse!

Dinosaur Provincial Park

Did you know Dinosaur Provincial Park became a park in 1955? Dinosaur Provincial Park is in the Alberta badlands. Badlands describe dry land with lots of hills covered with funny shaped rocks. At the park, you can hike, camp, and learn about dinosaurs and fossils.

Dinosaur Provincial Park was made to keep the dinosaur fossils safe. Dinosaur Provincial Park has fossils of almost 300 kinds of plants and animals. Check out the following Internet site for more information:

www.virtuallydirtuallydrumheller.com

Write two sentences about Dinosaur Provincial Park.

_____

_____

_____

_____

The CN Tower

Did you know the CN Tower is the tallest building in the world? CN stands for Canadian National. The CN Tower is in Toronto Ontario, and took three years to build. The CN Tower opened to visitors in 1976.

The CN Tower was built to be an antenna for radio and television stations. The CN Tower is 553 metres tall.

Inside the CN Tower, there is a glass floor. People can stand, sit or lie down on the glass floor and look at the city below.

The CN Tower has a special restaurant called the 360 Restaurant. It is the highest restaurant in the world. The 360 Restaurant is special because it rotates around the building. It takes seventy-two minutes for the restaurant to turn around once. This helps visitors to view the city of Toronto.

Niagara Falls

Did you know Niagara Falls is one of the most famous falls in the world? Many people from around the world come to Niagara Falls, Ontario to see the falls. Niagara Falls is on the Niagara River and is fifty-two metres tall. There are two ways to see Niagara Falls up close. The first way is to go "under the falls" through a tunnel that takes visitors to a sight seeing point very near the water. The second way is to take "The Maid of the Mist" boat, which carries visitors close to the falls.

Use different colours of blue crayons to colour Niagara Falls. Draw in "The Maid of the Mist" boat.

Klondike Gold Rush

Did you know that in 1896, gold was discovered in the Yukon? This very exciting time is known as the Klondike Gold Rush. Many people traveled to the Yukon to search for gold. These people were called gold prospectors.

Some people mined for gold. Some people panned for gold. They would scoop up the gold and dirt that washed down the river into pans. Then swished the water from the pan until the soil washed out and the gold stayed behind. In this activity, pretend to pan for gold.

What you need:
- Tub full of water
- Tub full of dirt
- Rocks and pebbles painted gold
- Tin foil plates

What you do:
1. Mix the rocks and pebbles in the tub of dirt.
2. Place a handful of dirt into the tin foil plate.
3. Scoop water into the plate over the tub of water.
4. Swirl the water around, spilling some of the dirt until the golden rocks and pebbles appear!

Canadian Animal Diorama

Create a diorama using the Canadian animal pictures below, along with your drawings.

What you need:
- Shoe, Kleenex or similar box
- Assorted colours of construction paper and picture cutouts
- Glue
- Scissors

What to do:
1. Paint a scene in the inside of the box.
2. Let dry and add construction paper details in the form of animals, birds, insects, etc.
3. This should be a three-dimensional representation of a place in Canada.

Name _____

Canadian Animal Diorama

Create a diorama using the Canadian animal pictures below along with your drawings.

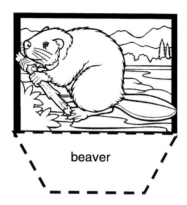

beaver

moose

bear

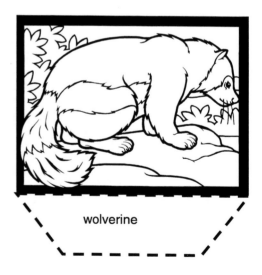

wolverine

Canadian Animal Word Search

beaver	bald eagle	cod	whale	great gray owl
caribou	buffalo	osphrey	lobster	Canada goose
blue jay	moose	lynx	muskrat	salmon
fox	deer	cougar	duck	polar bear

B	A	L	D	E	A	G	L	E	C	C	G
E	B	U	F	F	A	L	O	M	A	O	R
R	E	T	Q	U	P	D	S	U	N	U	E
C	A	R	I	B	O	U	P	S	A	G	A
S	V	S	T	D	L	C	H	K	D	A	T
B	E	A	G	E	A	K	R	R	A	R	G
L	R	L	G	E	R	Z	E	A	G	H	R
U	S	M	D	R	B	W	Y	T	O	U	A
E	M	O	O	S	E	C	O	D	O	P	Y
J	Z	N	W	H	A	L	E	J	S	Y	O
A	L	Y	N	X	R	F	O	X	E	R	W
Y	O	I	E	L	O	B	S	T	E	R	L

Draw your favourite
Canadian animal.

My favourite animal is

_____

GeoWat innovative teacher publishing inc. ©2003

Name _____

Popular Sports in Canada Word Search

skiing   hockey   tennis   soccer
lacrosse curling   swimming   baseball
basketball football golf   tobogganing
snowshoeing   skating

B	T	L	A	C	R	O	S	S	E	U	S
A	T	S	O	C	C	E	R	W	V	S	N
S	O	S	K	I	I	N	G	I	C	K	O
K	B	T	E	N	N	I	S	M	U	A	W
E	O	T	H	S	A	X	Y	M	R	T	S
T	G	G	O	L	F	M	H	I	L	I	H
B	G	W	C	Z	F	N	H	N	I	N	O
A	A	Q	K	R	I	O	L	G	N	G	E
L	N	T	E	H	I	K	I	N	G	O	I
L	I	W	Y	P	Y	T	E	S	F	G	N
T	N	F	O	O	T	B	A	L	L	B	G
T	G	B	A	S	E	B	A	L	L	A	U

My favourite sport is _____.

Canada Themed Art Crafts

- **Create a maple leaf wreath.** The maple leaf is a symbol of Canada and is on the flag of Canada. Have children trace the maple leaf tracers on red construction paper. Next, have children paste the maple leaves around a paper plate. Encourage the children to overlap the maple leaves for a fuller look. In the centre of the paper plate, paste a poem or picture about Canada.

- **Create a Canada collage.** Have children cutout pictures from magazines, newspapers or travel brochures to cut and paste into a collage. Try different Canada collage themes like food grown in Canada, animals of Canada or symbols of Canada.

- **Create a pair of "snowshoes".** Have children work in partners. One partner traces the outline of their partner's foot while standing on heavy cardboard. Then each child measures an oval about 20 cm around the outlines of their feet. Cut out the oval shapes. Next, punch out holes for the children on opposite sides of the arch area. Demonstrate for children how to lace each "snowshoe" with strong yarn. Now the children can step into their "snowshoes" with their shoes on and lace up to try them out!

- **Create a Canadian forest scene.** Demonstrate for children how to cut out different lengths of tree trunks from brown construction paper. Encourage children to add branches to their tree trunks. Next, glue the tree trunks onto white or manila paper. Then, tear green shades of tissue paper into small pieces for leaves. Lastly, carefully paste tissue paper leaves onto the tree branches.

Name _____

Concentration Playing Cards

Use the cards to match the picture of the province or territory to its name and flag.

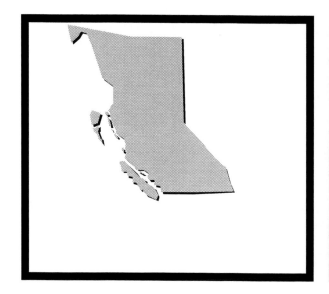

British Columbia

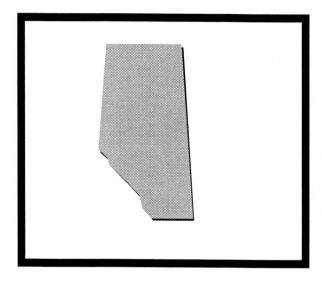

Alberta

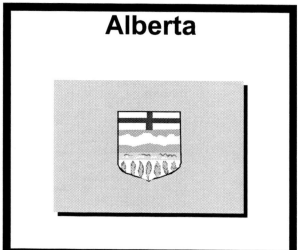

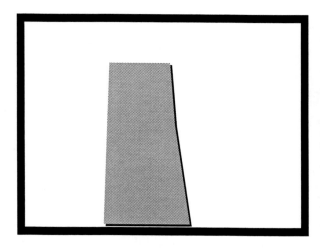

Saskatchewan

GeoWat innovative teacher publishing inc. ©2003

72

Concentration Playing Cards

Use the cards to match the picture of the province or territory to its name and flag.

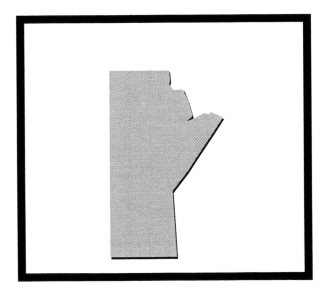

Manitoba

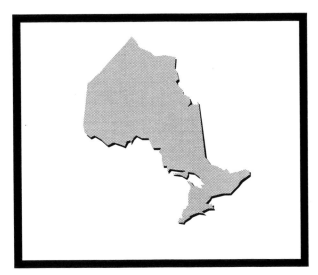

Ontario

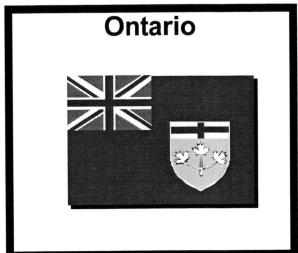

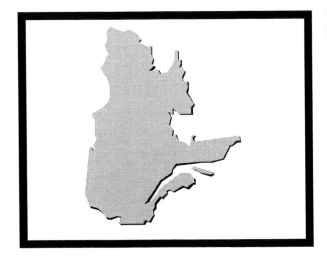

Quebec

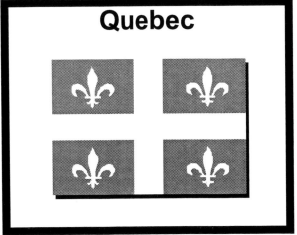

Name _____

Concentration Playing Cards

Use the cards to match the picture of the province or territory to its name and flag.

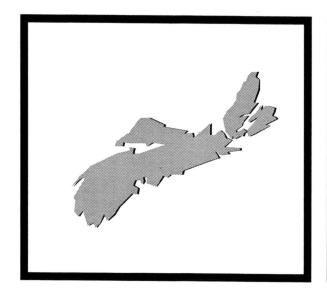

Nova Scotia

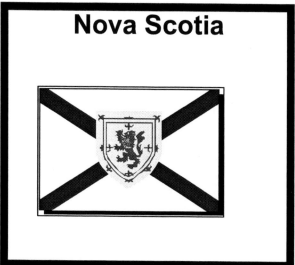

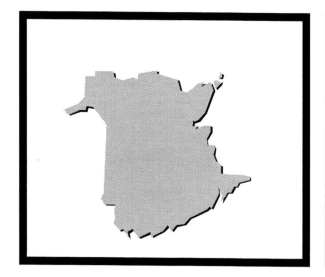

New Brunswick

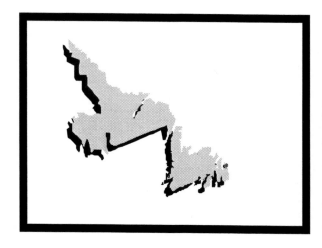

Newfoundland and Labrador

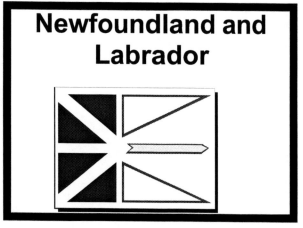

GeoWat innovative teacher publishing inc. ©2003

Concentration Playing Cards

Use the cards to match the picture of the province or territory to its name and flag.

Prince Edward Island

Nunavut

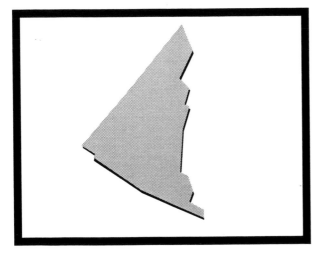

Yukon

Name _____

Concentration Playing Cards

Use the cards to match the picture of the province or territory to its name and flag.

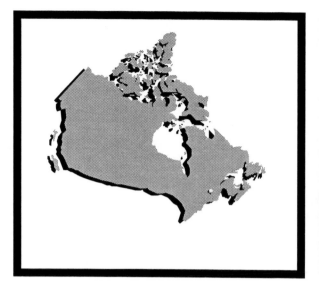

Canada

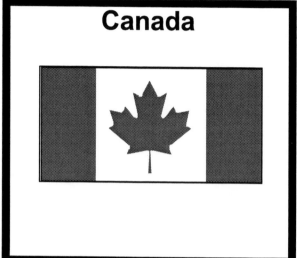

Northwest Territories

Some Canadian Holidays & Celebrations

Special Days in Canada

January 1st	New Year's Day
February 14th	St. Valentine's Day
February 15th	National Flag Day
March 17th	St. Patrick's Day
April 1st	April Fool's Day
May 24th	Victoria Day
July 1st	Canada Day
September 1st	Labour Day
October (First Monday)	Thanksgiving
October 31st	Halloween
November 1st	All Saints Day
December 25th	Christmas
December 26th	Boxing Day
December 31st	New Year's Eve

Special Days in the Provinces & Territories

Ontario	Civic Holiday [first Monday of August]
Quebec	National Day [June 24]
Nova Scotia	Natal Day [first Monday, August, except in Halifax where it varies from year to year, [usually Aug or July]
New Brunswick	New Brunswick Day [First Monday, Aug]
Manitoba	Civic Holiday [first Monday, Aug]
British Columbia	British Columbia Day [first Monday, Aug}
Prince Edward Island	Natal Day [usually on first Monday of Aug]
Saskatchewan	Civic Holiday [first Monday of Aug]
Alberta	Alberta Family Day [third Monday of Feb] Heritage Day [first Monday of Aug]
Newfoundland & Labrador	Celebrated on nearest Monday: St. George's Day [Apr. 23] Discovery Day [June 24] Memorial Day [July 1] Orangemen's Day [July 12] Regatta Day / Civic Holiday [fixed by municipal council orders]
Northwest Territories	Civic Holiday [first Monday of Aug]
Yukon	Discovery Day [third Monday of Aug]
Nunavut	Nunavut Day [July 9] Civic Holiday [first Monday in Aug]

GeoWat innovative teacher publishing inc. ©2003

Name _____

Rubric for Student Self-Assessment

	WOW	✓ I completed my work independently on time and with care. ✓ I added details and followed the instructions without help. ✓ I understand and can talk about what I have learned.
A		
B	**BRAVO**	✓ I completed my work on time and with care. ✓ I followed the instructions with almost no help. ✓ I understand and can talk about what I have learned.
C	**OKAY**	✓ I completed my work. ✓ I followed the instructions with some help. ✓ I understand and can talk about most of what I have learned.
D	**UH-OH**	✓ I need to complete my work on time and with care. ✓ I should ask for help when I need it. ✓ I understand and can talk about a few of the things that I have learned.

Name _____

Student Assessment Rubric

	Level One	Level Two	Level Three	Level Four
BASIC CONCEPTS	▪ Shows little of understanding of concepts ▪ Rarely gives complete explanations ▪ Teacher support is intensive	▪ Shows some understanding of concepts. ▪ Gives appropriate, but incomplete explanations ▪ Some teacher assistance is needed	▪ Shows understanding of most concepts. ▪ Usually gives complete or nearly complete explanations. ▪ Infrequent teacher support is needed	▪ Shows understanding of all or almost all concepts ▪ Consistently gives appropriate and complete explanations independently ▪ No teacher support is needed
COMMUNICATION	▪ Rarely communicates with clarity and precision in written and oral work ▪ Rarely uses appropriate terminology and vocabulary ▪ Intensive teacher prompts needed to use correct vocabulary	▪ Sometimes communicates with clarity and precision in written and oral work ▪ Rarely uses appropriate terminology and vocabulary ▪ Occasional teacher prompts needed to use correct vocabulary	▪ Usually communicates with clarity and precision in written and oral work ▪ Usually uses appropriate terminology and vocabulary ▪ Infrequent teacher prompts needed to use correct vocabulary	▪ Consistently communicates with clarity and precision in written and oral work with supporting details ▪ Consistently uses appropriate terminology and vocabulary ▪ No teacher prompts needed to use correct vocabulary
CONCEPT APPLICATION	▪ Student displays little understanding of connecting and comparing provinces and territories ▪ Rarely applies concepts and skills in a variety of contexts ▪ Intensive teacher support is needed to encourage application of concepts	▪ Student sometimes displays understanding of connecting and comparing provinces and territories ▪ Sometimes applies concepts and skills in a variety of contexts ▪ Occasional teacher support is needed to encourage application of concepts	▪ Student usually displays understanding of connecting and comparing provinces and territories ▪ Usually applies concepts and skills in a variety of contexts ▪ Infrequent teacher support is needed to encourage application of concepts	▪ Student consistently displays understanding of comparing provinces and territories ▪ Almost always applies concepts and skills in a variety of contexts ▪ No teacher support is needed to encourage application of concepts

All About Canada Expert

Great Work!

Canadian Expert

Quality Worker